MAGNETS

SCIENCE SECRETS

Jason Cooper

The Rourke Corporation, Inc.
Vero Beach, Florida 32964

Edited by Sandra A. Robinson

PHOTO CREDITS

© Lynn M. Stone: cover, title page, pages 4, 7, 8, 10, 12, 13, 15,
18; courtesy Fermilab Visual Media Services, page 17;
courtesy NASA, page 21

LIBRARY OF CONGRESS
Library of Congress Cataloging-in-Publication Data
Cooper, Jason, 1942-
   Magnets / by Jason Cooper.
   p. cm. — (Science secrets)
   Includes index.
   Summary: Provides a simple discussion of natural magnetic
force, electromagnets, and magnetic fields.
   ISBN 0-86593-165-8
   1. Magnetism — Juvenile literature. [1. Magnetism.]
I. Title. II. Series: Cooper, Jason, 1942-   Science secrets.
QC753.7.C66   1992
538—dc20   92-8807
                    CIP
                    AC

Printed in the USA

TABLE OF CONTENTS

MAGNETISM

We often use such things as nails, screws or glue to make objects cling tightly together. **Magnetism,** however, makes some objects hold to each other all by themselves.

Magnetism is a natural force that pushes and pulls. It works between objects known as magnets. Magnets can pull other magnets and certain other metal objects.

Can opener magnet lifts can lid

THE MAGNET'S FORCE

Magnetism is an **invisible** force—a force that you cannot see. That force causes some metal objects, like those made of iron, to stick to the magnet.

Common magnets, for example, will cling to a refrigerator or a car door. They will also hold on to pins, nails, paper clips and many other objects. However, a magnet's force does not pull paper, wood or plastic.

*Paper clips collect on
a horseshoe magnet*

THE MAGNET'S POLES

The bar magnet is a common type of magnet. (It has the shape of a candy bar.) Its pull is more powerful at its ends, or **poles,** than along its middle.

One pole is called the north pole. The other is the south pole. The north pole of one magnet will attract another magnet's south pole. The same poles of different magnets, when facing, will resist each other.

Magnet's pole attracts iron shavings

MAGNET ROCKS

Hundreds of years ago the only magnets were those found in the ground. They were known as lodestones or magic stones. People were amazed by the lodestones' power to stick to metal.

Today we know lodestone as magnetite, a type of iron. Lodestone is naturally **magnetic.** That is, magnetite has a magnet's pull.

Magnetite

Two-thousand-pound electromagnet

Magnetized letters

MAGNET SHAPES

Magnetite is rough and jagged, as nature made it. But today we build magnets in many shapes and sizes.

Some magnets are as fine as dust! Some weigh thousands of pounds.

Magnets may be round, barshaped, or shaped like thick saucers. Some bar magnets are bent into horseshoe shapes. Each type has a use of its own.

*Horseshoe-shaped magnet
with iron shavings*

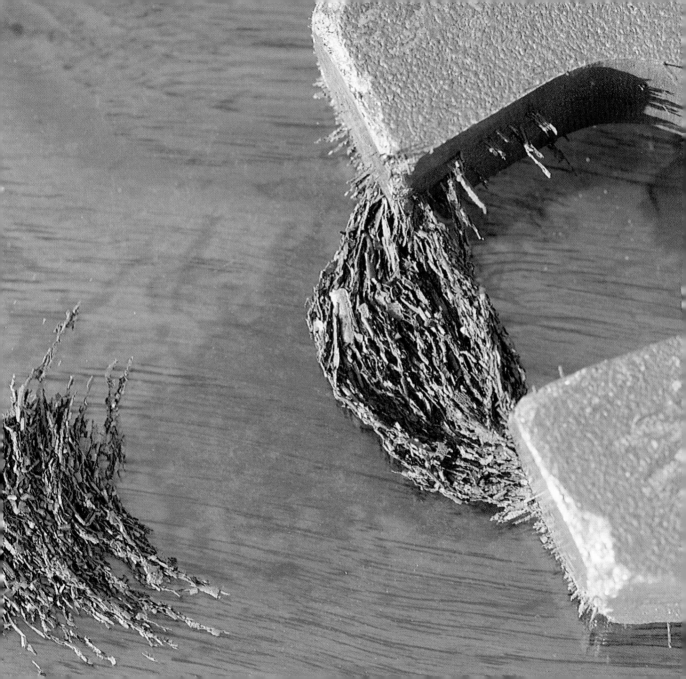

MAGNETS AT WORK

Magnets are used in many important ways. Magnets help computers, telephones, electric motors and many other inventions to work.

Magnets are used in homes, factories, hospitals, laboratories and other places.

The magnetic **compass** uses a magnet to tell which way someone is going—north, south, east or west.

Magnets at work in the Fermi National Accelerator Laboratory

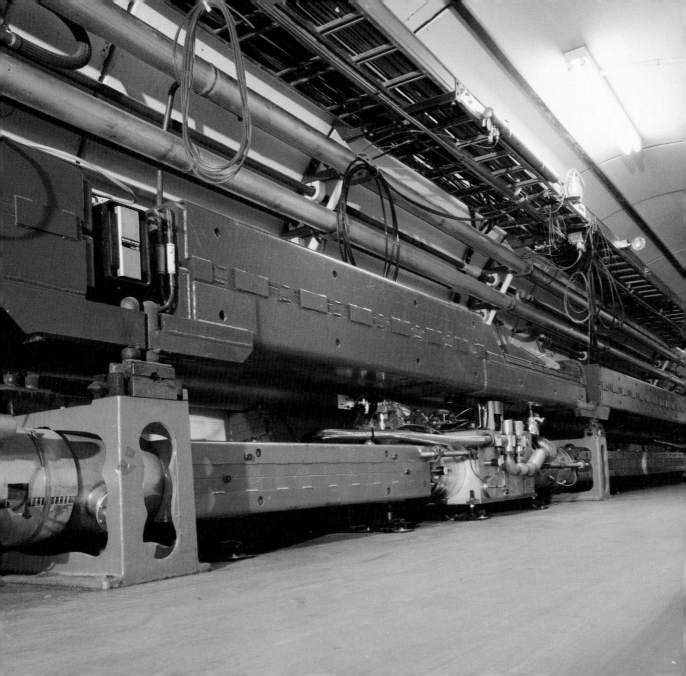

MAGNETS WITH ELECTRICITY

Magnets that use electricity are called **electromagnets.** This type of magnet can be turned on and off, just like an electric light bulb.

Some electromagnets are made to lift heavy metal objects, such as scrap iron. When the electric current is turned off, the magnet loses its pull, or magnetism. Then the object the magnet is carrying is released.

Electromagnet releasing scrap iron

THE MAGNET EARTH

The earth has magnetic poles, too. Scientists believe that much of the earth's **core,** or center, is made up of magnetic materials.

The north magnetic pole is at the "top" of the world in northern Canada. The south magnetic pole is at the "bottom" of the earth in Antarctica.

The earth's magnetic pull makes the magnetic needle of a compass line up north and south.

Planet earth: our largest magnet

THE MAGNETIC FIELD

You do not have to put your nose into a rose blossom to smell the rose. The scent of the flower reaches into the air nearby.

Imagine a magnet is a rose and its **magnetic field** is the scent. A magnetic field surrounds each magnet like a flower's scent. The magnetic field is the area around the magnet in which its force is present.

Glossary

compass (KUMP us) — an instrument using a magnetic needle to tell direction

core (KORE) — the center or inner part

electromagnet (e LEK tro MAG net) — a magnet that operates with an electric current and can be turned on and off

invisible (in VIZ ah bull) — unable to be seen by the naked eye

magnetic (mag NET ik) — that which has the pulling or pushing force of a magnet

magnetic field (mag NET ik FEELD) — the area surrounding a magnet in which the magnet's force is present

magnetism (MAG nuht ism) — the invisible pushing or pulling force of magnets

pole (POLE) — the point of highest attraction, such as the opposite end of the earth or of certain types of magnets

INDEX